ROMAN
MYTHS AND
LEGENDS

Jilly Hunt

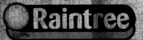

Chicago, Illinois

Edited by Nancy Dickmann, Adam Miller, and
Claire Throp
Designed by Jo Hinton-Malivoire
Original illustrations © Capstone Global Library,
Ltd. 2013
Illustrations by Xöul
Picture research by Hannah Taylor
Production by Victoria Fitzgerald
Originated by Capstone Global Library, Ltd.
Printed and bound in China by Leo Paper
Products, Ltd.

16 15 14 13 12
10 9 8 7 6 5 4 3 2 1

**Library of Congress Cataloging-in-
Publication Data**
Hunt, Jilly.
Roman myths and legends / Jilly Hunt.
p. cm.—(All about myths)
Includes bibliographical references and index.
ISBN 978-1-4109-4974-5—ISBN 978-1-4109-4979-
0 (pbk.)
1. Mythology, Roman—Juvenile literature. 2. Gods,
Roman—Juvenile literature. I. Title.

BL803.H86 2013
398.20937—dc23   2012017720

Acknowledgments
We would like to thank the following for
permission to reproduce photographs: Alamy
Images pp. 5 (© Jozef Sedmak), 6 (© Picture
Contact BV), 8 (© WoodyStock), 10 (© B&Y
Photography), 21, 26 (© AF archive); Corbis pp.
4 (Nathan Benn), 7 (Adam Woolfitt), 9 (Mimmo
Jodice), 11, 19 (Araldo de Luca), 16 (Jose Fuste
Raga), 39 (Burstein Collection); Getty Images p. 23
(Alinari Archives); Press Association p. 35 (Italian
Cultural Ministry); Shutterstock pp. 17 (© nhtg),
20 (© Vladimir Korostyshevskiy), 22, 40 (© Philip
Lange), 34 (© Anthony Smith); Superstock pp. 12
(Photoservice Electa), 27 (Piotr Ciesla), 29 (The
Art Archive), 41 (Science Faction); The Art Archive
pp. 13 (Museo Nazionale Palazzo Altemps Rome/
Dagli Orti), 18 (Musee du Louvre Paris/Gianni
Dagli Orti), 28, 38 (Dagli Orti).

Background images: Shutterstock (©tanais),
(©vapy), (©imagestalk), (©Olga Matseyko),
(©I. Pilon), (©toadberry), (©pashabo), (©Maugli),
(©Robert Adrian Hillman), (©Anna Omelchenko),
(©gallimaufry), (©Brian Weed), (©Vangelis76),
(©Elenamiv).

Cover photograph of Hercules wearing the lion
skin reproduced with permission of Shutterstock
(© Vladimir Korostyshevskiy). Cover graphic:
Shutterstock (© Martin Capek).

The publisher would like to thank Alex Smith,
Senior Research Fellow in Archaeology at the
University of Reading, for his invaluable assistance
in the production of this book.

Every effort has been made to contact copyright
holders of any material reproduced in this book.
Any omissions will be rectified in subsequent
printings if notice is given to the publisher.

Contents

Did you know?

Discover some interesting facts about Roman myths.

Who's who?

Find out more about some of the main characters in Roman myths.

MYTH LINKS

Learn about similar characters or stories from other cultures.

What Are Myths and Legends?

Throughout history, humans have told stories. Some stories are about the creation of the world. Others are about powerful gods and goddesses, or heroes and tricksters and their many quests. These myths and legends have been handed down from generation to generation. The stories have been changed and added to with each generation.

EXPLAINING THE WORLD

Today, scientists can explain the origins of our universe, but in ancient history, mythology was used to explain things instead. Myths are traditional stories often used to help people understand the world and how they should live. Most people no longer think of myths as being factually correct, but at the time people really believed in them.

This is a mosaic of the Roman god Apollo. It is part of a floor decoration in a 4th century CE Roman villa.

THE ANCIENT ROMANS

The ancient Romans started out as a small tribe of people who lived in what is now Italy over 3,000 years ago. A small cluster of villages eventually grew into the big city of Rome. Rome fought many wars and conquered many people, until large areas of Europe, Africa, and Asia were under Roman rule. The ancient Romans forced their religious beliefs on the people they conquered, and so their myths spread.

Who's who?

We know about the early history of Rome from the writings of Roman historians such as Livy. Livy moved to Rome in about 29 BCE and started to write the story of the city. Some of his stories are based on myths and folktales. He was the first person to record Roman history in personal and moral terms rather than in terms of politics.

For how to pronounce Roman names, see pages 42–43.

Myths from Many Cultures

Many Roman myths have come from other cultures. As the Roman Empire expanded, the Romans discovered new gods. They incorporated these gods into their beliefs. For example, many Roman males worshiped the god Mithras, whose cult originated from Persia (now Iran). In other cases, a Roman god might be combined with a god from another culture. For example, Sulis Minerva was a goddess worshiped in Roman Britain. Sulis was a Celtic goddess of healing and sacred waters, and Minerva was the Roman goddess of wisdom.

ETRUSCAN MYTHS

The Etruscans lived in northern Italy before the Romans. Many aspects of their culture were adopted by the Romans. For example, many Roman gods, such as Saturn and Diana, were originally Etruscan.

The goddess Sulis Minerva is associated with the Roman baths at Bath in England.

Did you know?

The ancient Romans believed that the gods were like people but with special powers. The gods were members of a family and, just like normal people, they got married, had children, quarreled, and fought. The Romans believed that the gods would live forever and so were immortal, whereas normal people were mortal.

Who's who?

Mithras was the god of light and is known for slaying the cosmic bull. We are not sure why he slayed the bull. Some people think the bull's blood spilled on the ground and made the soil fertile. The religion of Mithraism promised life after death, making it popular with Roman soldiers. However, its followers were sworn to secrecy, so we don't know much about it.

This stone sculpture shows Mithras slaying the cosmic bull.

GODS FOR EVERYTHING

Romans were not only superstitious about big issues like life and death, but were also concerned with everyday issues, like bread-making. Romans had spirits, gods, and goddesses for every part of life.

Who's who?

Janus was the god of doorways and of good beginnings. The month January is named after him. He is often shown with two faces: one looking forward and one looking back.

HOUSEHOLD GODS

To protect their homes, each Roman family worshiped protector gods called the Lares. These twins were the sons of Mercury, the messenger of the gods, and Lara. The Lares were worshiped at an altar in the home called a *lararium*. Lares could protect any place so are also associated with crossroads and fields.

The Romans also worshiped a pair of gods called the Penates. The Penates were gods of the larder or table. Food was put in front of the statues in the *lararium* at the start of every meal as an offering to the Penates.

VESTA

Vesta was the goddess of the fire in the hearth. Since fire was hard to make in ancient Rome, Vesta was very important. She was worshiped in the home and also had a temple dedicated to her in Rome. In this temple, there was a flame which was always to be kept alight.

Roman families held daily prayers and gave offerings of food and wine to please the gods at the household shrine.

Did you know?

According to myth, the Lares would borrow the dogs of the goddess of hunting, Diana, and together would chase away any thieves from the home.

Gods and Goddesses

When the Romans conquered the ancient Greeks, they discovered a whole new group of gods and goddesses to add to their own. However, the Romans changed the name of the Greek gods just to show who was in power. Sometimes, they combined the Greek god's attributes with those of other Roman gods so that this god got new powers.

MYTH LINKS

Many gods were known by different names in different cultures.

GREEK NAME	ROMAN NAME
Zeus	Jupiter
Hera	Juno
Poseidon	Neptune
Hestia	Vesta
Ares	Mars
Athena	Minerva
Aphrodite	Venus
Hermes	Mercury
Artemis	Diana
Hephaestus	Vulcan
Apollo	Apollo
Hades/Pluto	Pluto

The Romans believed that Minerva sprung out of Jupiter's head, wearing full armor!

THE OLYMPIANS

There are many different characters in Greek mythology, but the most important group were the gods and goddesses who lived on Mount Olympus, called the Olympians. The Romans didn't seem to give Mount Olympus or the group another name, but the myth gradually changed into the gods living in the sky.

Zeus was the sky god to the Greeks, but the Romans blended his attributes with those of the Etruscan god of thunder, Tinia, and gave him the Roman name Jupiter. Jupiter became the supreme ruler of the gods.

GODDESSES

The next two most powerful rulers were the two goddesses Juno and Minerva. Juno was the wife of Jupiter and was the goddess of marriage and childbirth. Minerva was the goddess of wisdom, and her attributes were blended with the Greek goddess Athena. In mythology, she is the daughter of Jupiter.

Jupiter destroyed his enemies with thunderbolts. Here he is about to hurl a thunderbolt in a fight with the Giants. Jupiter is often shown with an eagle who holds the thunderbolts in his claws.

GODS OF WAR AND FIRE

Mars was the god of war and son of the goddess Juno. The Roman poet Ovid tells a myth that Juno was jealous of Jupiter after he created Minerva without a mother. Juno wanted to create a child without a father. She asked for help from another goddess and created Mars all by herself.

Vulcan was the god of fire. He was a blacksmith, and his forge was believed to be under Mount Etna, a volcano in Sicily, Italy. Vulcan was the father of a fire-breathing monster called Cacus, and he was married to Venus, the goddess of love.

Who's who?

Ovid was born in 43 BCE. He is famous for his long poem *Metamorphoses,* which is a collection of myths.

Venus is mother of Cupid, the god of love, and of Aeneas, the ancestor of the Romans.

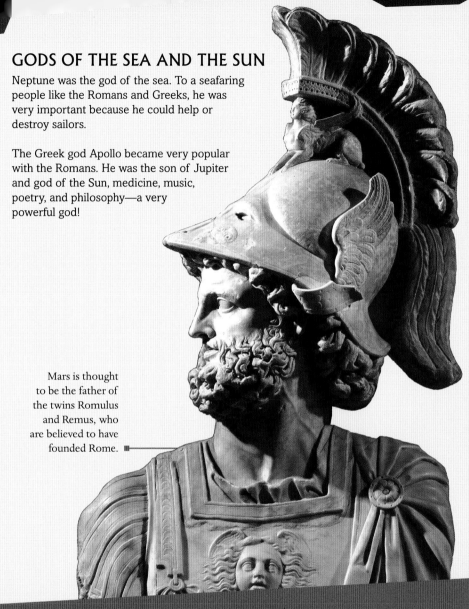

GODS OF THE SEA AND THE SUN

Neptune was the god of the sea. To a seafaring people like the Romans and Greeks, he was very important because he could help or destroy sailors.

The Greek god Apollo became very popular with the Romans. He was the son of Jupiter and god of the Sun, medicine, music, poetry, and philosophy—a very powerful god!

Mars is thought to be the father of the twins Romulus and Remus, who are believed to have founded Rome.

MYTH LINKS

In ancient Greek mythology, the god of the underworld was an important figure. He was called Hades but the Greeks thought it was unlucky to say his name, so they called him by other names, one of which was Pluto. The Romans adopted this god and called him Pluto.

Vulcan and the golden throne

"Let her go!" bellowed Vulcan as he saw his mother, Juno, dangling from the heavens by a golden chain. Jupiter had hung her there as a punishment after an argument.

"You stay out of this, son!" hissed Jupiter. He grabbed Vulcan's foot and hurled him out of the heavens.

Vulcan's fall to Earth took a whole day and night. It would have killed a mortal man but merely left the god with a leg injury that caused him to limp.

Deep under Mount Etna, Vulcan sulked. "Where is my mother? Does she not care enough to see if I'm hurt?" he asked Cyclops, the one-eyed giant. "I'll show her that she can't treat me this way."

Vulcan and Cyclops set about building a beautiful golden throne for Juno—but this was a throne with a difference. Vulcan carefully fitted it with hidden springs that would hold her firmly in place. "She'll never escape now," said Vulcan, smiling craftily. "She'll be sorry."

Juno was delighted with the gift of her golden throne and admired its beauty as she sat down. Of course, as soon as she was seated on the throne the hidden springs sprang into action and Juno was held prisoner.

"Sit still, Juno!" Jupiter snapped. "Vulcan's played a trick on you. Tell Mercury to bring him here immediately."

But Vulcan was not going to be swayed by this smooth-talking messenger.

"Send Bacchus, the god of wine then!" ordered Jupiter.

Now, forges are hot places and Vulcan was thirsty after a hard day's work, so he welcomed Bacchus's offering of wine.

"Vulcan! Where have you been?" Juno scolded as Vulcan limped into her palace. "Release me at once and you had better apologize to your father too. He's furious with you."

Vulcan freed his mother and asked forgiveness from his father, but he refused to come back to heaven, preferring to live in the sooty darkness of his forge.

Worshiping Gods and Goddesses

The ancient Romans built special buildings, called temples, for worshiping their gods and goddesses. Inside a temple was a statue of the god. People would make offerings of food, flowers, or money in front of the statue.

The Romans would pray to a particular god depending on what they wanted good luck or protection for. For example, Ceres was the goddess of crops and harvests. During a time of grain shortage, the Romans built a temple to Ceres, to try to protect against a famine.

WHAT REMAINS TODAY

We know about Roman temples because some of them, or their remains, survive today. The Capitoline Temple buildings were built to worship Juno, Jupiter, and Minerva on the Capitoline Hill in Rome. This was an important site in ancient Rome.

Did you know?

The Romans believed that killing a valuable animal would show how important they thought the gods were. A priest would perform the sacrifice on an altar outside the temple. The Romans believed that the internal organs of the sacrificed animals could show them the wishes of the gods and tell the future.

These temples in Tunisia were built for Juno, Jupiter, and Minerva.

Did you know?

The gods and goddesses of a culture are sometimes called a pantheon. The word "pantheon" comes from the Greek and means "all gods." In Rome, there is a temple to all the gods that is also called the Pantheon. Its dome was the largest in the ancient world and measured 140 feet (43 meters) across!

FESTIVALS

The Romans held festivals to honor their gods and goddesses. There were a lot of Roman gods, so there were a lot of festivals! Hundreds were celebrated each year.

NEW YEAR

The Romans originally started their new year on March 1, which marked the start of 19 days of dancing and feasting. Starting in 153 BCE, the Roman new year was moved to January 1. On this day, there was a festival to thank Jupiter for his protection over the past year. Bulls would be sacrificed to please him.

On August 13, a feast day was held to honor Diana, the goddess of hunting. Diana was believed to be the protector of the lower classes, so **slaves** would be given the day off.

■ The goddess Ceres is often shown with a crown of ears of corn, and her followers made offerings of corn.

SPORTING CONTESTS

Some festivals included sporting contests, called games. These games were seen as being another way of honoring a god or goddess. In April, the *Ludi Ceriales* games were held in praise of Ceres, the goddess of crops and harvests. It was a time of celebration and feasting.

TRADING PLACES

One of the most popular Roman festivals was held December 17–24. It was called *Saturnalia* in honor of the god Saturn. As well as sacrifices and games, masters and their slaves would switch places for a while!

Heroes, Tricksters, and Thieves

The Romans also told stories about heroes. Many of the heroes were the child of a god and a human. Being the child of a god gave the heroes powers beyond that of normal humans. The heroes embarked on many fantastic adventures. Some were worshiped as gods.

HERCULES

One of the most popular heroes in Roman mythology was Hercules. Hercules was known for his strength, and the most famous stories are about his 12 "labors." These are the 12 tasks that he was given as punishment for killing his own children. Hercules's tasks included feats of strength and skill, such as killing the Nemean lion and capturing a dangerous bull that belched flames.

The Hercules story about the Nemean lion has similarities with the Christian story of Samson and the lion, in which Samson rips apart a lion with his bare hands.

■ The Disney film *Hercules* is based on the Greek and Roman myths of Hercules.

Who's who?

Gaius Mucius Scaevola is a legendary Roman hero who saved Rome from attack in 508 BCE. He was caught in the enemy's camp trying to kill the king. He was going to be tortured, but he was released when he put his right hand into a fire to show that he had no fear.

Did you know?

Roman emperors were just ordinary humans. However, after his death in 14 CE, Emperor Augustus was made a god. It was just a sign of respect, but many later emperors were worshiped as gods after their deaths. However, the slightly insane Emperor Caligula actually believed he was a god.

PLAYING TRICKS

Some mythological characters are tricksters. They may play tricks, steal, or break the rules in other ways. Yet despite their naughtiness, they may be quite inventive and do things that help humans. Tricksters can be the heroes of some stories.

Prometheus is one such figure. His stories were taken by the Romans from Greek mythology. In one story, Prometheus taught humans how to trick the gods into feasting on bones and fat as sacrifices, instead of tender meat. When he found out, Jupiter took fire away from humans as punishment. Fire was an essential part of everyday life, so Prometheus stole it back and returned it to humans.

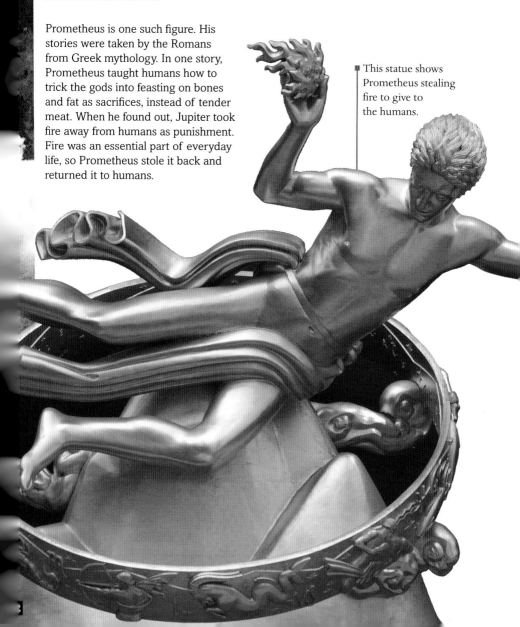

This statue shows Prometheus stealing fire to give to the humans.

Did you know?

After Prometheus stole fire from the gods, he was punished by being chained to a rock. Every day, an eagle would come and eat his liver, but it would grow back to be eaten again the next day.

Mercury is often shown with winged sandals for speedy traveling and his magic wand that could make people fall asleep.

THE GOD OF THIEVES

The most famous of the Roman thieves and tricksters is Mercury. He was the son of Jupiter and the goddess Maia and acted as Jupiter's messenger. He was the god of commerce and thieves. It is said that on the day that he was born, he crept away from his sleeping mother and stole Apollo's cattle.

MYTH LINKS

Tricksters also appear in myths and legends from other cultures. For example, Brer Rabbit is popular in the folklore of American Indian and African peoples.

The theft of Apollo's cattle

The baby Mercury was not even a day old yet, and already he was tired of sitting on his mother's knee. "This is boring!" he squawked, as he jumped down. Rummaging around near her chair, he found an empty turtle shell lying on the ground.

"Now, what could I do with this shell?" he wondered. Struck by an idea, he made holes in the sides of the shell and stretched strings across it, then strummed them to make sweet music. He had invented the first lyre—not bad for a baby!

Soon Mercury began to feel hungry. "I want some food," he told his mother, but she was asleep. "I'll find something myself then," he muttered as he set off. Reaching a green meadow, he found it was full of fat, young cattle. They'd make a fine meal…if they didn't belong to the Sun god, Apollo.

Mercury looked around to see if the cattle were being watched and saw that Apollo was sleeping. Quietly, he led away 50 of Apollo's cattle, being careful to cover their tracks. Then he killed and ate two of them. Delicious!

Meanwhile, Apollo woke from his snooze and slowly sat up, rubbing his eyes. "Hey! Who's stolen my cattle?" he shouted, as he leaped to his feet to look for clues. Where could they be?

Then Apollo remembered: that morning he had heard an announcement that the god of thieves had been born. Could a baby be the thief? He went to track down Mercury's mother and found the baby asleep in his mother's arms.

"You can't fool me, Mercury!" said Apollo. He dragged Mercury off to Olympus to face the other gods, who found him guilty of the theft.

"I'm sorry," said Mercury. "Here, have this lyre to make up for it."

Apollo was so pleased with the lyre that he forgave Mercury and gave him a magic wand called a caduceus, which had the power to stop fighting.

Quests and Adventures

In Roman mythology, both mortals and gods and goddesses embark on adventures and quests. One tale that was important to the Romans was the Greek adventure of Jason and the Argonauts. A poet named Apollonius of Rhodes had written a long poem, the *Argonautica,* which told the story. It was later translated for the Romans.

The poem tells of the exciting adventures of Jason and his crew, who sailed in a boat called the *Argo*. They were sent to a faraway land to find the legendary Golden Fleece. On the way, they faced many challenges, such as sailing through the Clashing Rocks. These rocks would swing together and crush anything that passed through them.

The story of Jason and the Argonauts remains popular today, and has been made into a film.

MYTH LINKS

The Roman poet Gaius Valerius Flaccus also wrote an epic poem about the voyage of Jason and the Argonauts. It was based on Apollonius's work, but it showed the influences of Roman writers such as Virgil and Ovid.

Did you know?

When Jason selected his crew, he chose the best and strongest men he could find. Many of them were the sons of gods. Even Hercules was part of the crew!

CASTOR AND POLLUX

The twin brothers Castor and Pollux were part of Jason's crew. Castor's father was a mortal, but Jupiter was the father of Pollux. The Romans worshiped these twins and thought of them as heroes. They believed that one of the duties of Castor and Pollux was to look after those lost at sea and send out lights to guide sailors.

Castor and Pollux were often called upon by Romans at moments of crisis.

This picture of the Roman poet Virgil is from a manuscript of *The Aeneid* from the 5th century CE.

TROUBLESOME TWINS

Castor and Pollux were always fighting with each other and causing trouble. In one story they carried off two sisters, Phoebe and Hileira. The girls' cousins, Idas and Lynceus, came to rescue them and got into a fatal fight with Castor and Pollux. Idas killed Castor and Pollux killed Lynceus. Jupiter was furious, and in revenge killed Idas with a thunderbolt.

In some versions of the myths, Castor was mortal and Pollux (being Jupiter's son) was immortal. When Castor was killed, Jupiter let Pollux share his immortality with his brother, so that they wouldn't be separated. Castor and Pollux would spend alternate days in heaven (where they appear as the constellation Gemini) and the underworld.

Who's who?

The Roman poet Virgil wrote *Aeneid*, which retells the story of Aeneas and the founding of Rome. Virgil became famous in Rome, and his work was used in school textbooks.

Aeneas' mother, the goddess Venus, helps to keep him safe on his long journey.

THE QUEST FOR A NEW CITY

One of the most famous quests in Roman mythology is that of Aeneas. This marks the start of the adventure which leads to the founding of Rome. Aeneas is the son of the goddess Venus and Prince Anchises, and he fights to defend Troy against the Greeks. After the Trojan War, Aeneas followed the prophecy about him—that he would found a new city. He had many adventures, including escaping from the Cyclops, being shipwrecked, falling in love, and visiting the underworld, where he was shown a vision of the future: the city of Rome.

Aeneas and the fall of Troy

For 10 long years, the city of Troy had been at war with the Greeks. Finally, the Greeks pretended to go home, but left behind a giant wooden horse with soldiers hidden inside. At night, while the Trojans slept, the Greek soldiers crept out of their hiding place and attacked the city, killing everyone they found.

The Trojan warrior Aeneas had gone to bed, glad that the long war was over. But soon he was woken by the sound of fighting. "The city is on fire!" he exclaimed, looking out of his window. "I've got to warn the king."

Stumbling through smoke and rubble, Aeneas ripped off the armor from a dead Greek soldier and made his way to the palace. But it was too late—the king was dead.

Aeneas realized that the Greeks would destroy the city. His thoughts turned to his family. "We must escape!" he thought. He battled his way home, killing enemy soldiers as he passed through the burning streets.

"We must leave immediately," Aeneas ordered as he arrived home.

"I can't go, son. I am old and crippled," Anchises told him.

"I'm not leaving you, Father. I can carry you," pleaded Aeneas.

As Anchises looked over at his grandson, he saw a strange light hovering about his head. This was a sign from the gods that his family would survive. He climbed onto Aeneas's back, clutching the statues of the household gods.

Arriving at the safety of the harbor, Aeneas looked back. His wife was no longer with them. He rushed back to find her spirit waiting for him. "Go on without me, and head for the banks of the River Tiber," the spirit whispered.

Aeneas returned to the harbor and prepared to set sail. Other Trojans, who had escaped the burning city, came to join him on his adventure. There was a fleet of many ships ready to set sail.

Continued on page 32

Stormy waters

"They'll not get away that easily!" the goddess Juno cried. She hated the Trojans and had taken the side of the Greeks in the war. She whipped up an enormous storm, but the commotion woke the sea god, Neptune.

"How dare you interfere in my seas, Juno! Waters, be calm!" he ordered angrily. It was just in time to save Aeneas and his crew, but several ships were wrecked. Aeneas headed for the nearest port, Carthage, in North Africa.

Aeneas soon fell in love with Dido, the queen of Carthage. They seemed so in love that the gods thought Aeneas had forgotten about the prophecy. Mercury came to remind him. "I haven't forgotten, but I must go in secret," replied Aeneas. He knew that Dido would not want him to go.

Dido awoke one morning to see the last of Aeneas's ships leaving. "Burn all his things!" ordered the heartbroken queen. As the flames licked around Aeneas's possessions, Dido leaped into the pyre and plunged a dagger into her heart.

Anchises, who had died on the way to Carthage, soon appeared to his son in a vision. "You must travel to Cumae to meet the Sibyl," he instructed. The Sibyl of Cumae was a priestess who could predict the future. She led Aeneas down into the underworld.

"Watch out for Cerberus!" warned the Sibyl, as she tossed a piece of drugged cake to the three-headed guard dog. With fierce Cerberus asleep, the pair was able to continue to the Elysian Fields, where the souls of the good could rest forever. There they found the spirit of Anchises.

"You will found a new city, Rome," revealed Anchises. Aeneas tried to embrace his beloved father, but grabbed only air.

Aeneas hurried back to the world of the living and sailed up the coast of Italy. When he saw the mouth of the Tiber River he knew this was to be their new homeland.

The Beginning and the End

Every culture has stories telling about its origin. For the Romans, the founding of Rome was their important story. Roman historians, such as Livy, tell a story that combines a Greek myth with a Roman folktale. The hero Aeneas finally arrives in Italy, where he marries a princess and they start a family. It is Aeneas's descendants who are credited with founding the city of Rome.

The image of the she-wolf feeding Romulus and Remus was important to the Romans. They made many sculptures of the scene.

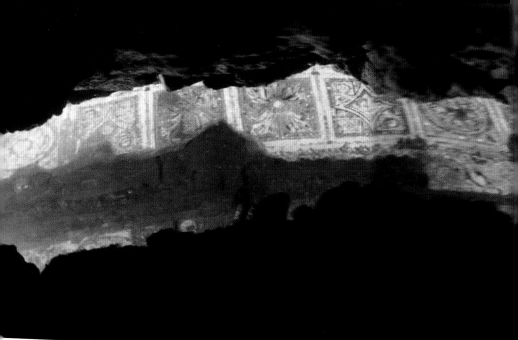

■ This cave might be where the Romans thought the she-wolf raised Romulus and Remus.

THE FOUNDING OF ROME

Twin boys named Romulus and Remus were born to an unmarried priestess named Rhea Silvia. She was the daughter of Numitor, who was a descendant of Aeneas. Rhea claimed that the twins' father was the god Mars. Because she was a priestess, she was to be killed as punishment for getting pregnant.

The baby boys were abandoned, to be swept away by the Tiber River. However, the boys were washed ashore and found by a friendly she-wolf. The wolf fed and cared for them with her own young, until one day they were found by a kindly shepherd. You can discover the rest of the tale on the next page.

Did you know?

In 2007, archaeologists discovered an underground Roman grotto. They think it might prove to be built on the site that the Romans thought was the cave of the she-wolf. Archaeologists say that this find shows that fictional myths can help the search for historical facts.

Romulus and Remus

Rhea Silvia was pregnant. But she was a priestess, and that wasn't allowed.

"What are we to do with her?" her father, Numitor, asked his wife. "The law says that she must be buried alive. Oh, the shame! And what about the babies?"

"She says they will be twin boys and the father is Mars!" replied his wife. "How could she do this? Does she not remember we are the descendants of Aeneas?"

Servants carried the babies to the river. They had been told to push the boys far out into the river, but the river was in full flood. "I'm not getting any closer," said one of them. "We'll leave them on the side."

The rushing river carried the basket downstream, but the babies didn't drown. The basket eventually snagged on a tree root close to the bank and was discovered by a she-wolf. The wolf looked after the boys alongside her own young, until one day they were found by Faustulus the shepherd, who took them home.

"They must be Rhea Silvia's boys," said his wife, when she heard Faustulus's story. "What will we do with them? We'll get in trouble if anyone knows they are alive."

Bravely, they decided to raise the children as their own, and the boys grew up to be strong and fearless.

"Let's build a new city!" the boys decided one day. But they had warrior blood in their veins and were constantly quarreling. As they were building the city wall, they fought about what to call this great city.

"We'll call it Reme," said Remus.

"No, it should be called Rome!" cried Romulus.

The quarreling turned into fighting. Remus jumped over the wall, bringing it crashing down. Romulus picked up a boulder and smashed it down on Remus's head, killing him. "All who try to leap the walls of Rome will die!" cried Romulus. Then he sobbed for the loss of his beloved brother.

END OF AN ERA

The Romans worshiped many different gods and goddesses, but in the Middle East the religions of Christianity and Judaism were growing. These religions had a single god, so their followers couldn't worship the Roman gods and goddesses, and more importantly, the emperors.

The Roman emperors didn't like this, so they persecuted the Christians and Jews living in the Roman Empire. Emperor Nero ordered hundreds of Christians to be ripped apart by wild animals because he thought they had made the gods angry and started a fire that burned down Rome. Later emperors executed thousands of Christians because they wouldn't give up their faith, and they tried to remove Judaism completely.

Did you know?

Christians would meet in secret locations—even in underground tunnels, which were usually used as burial vaults!

Before an important battle, Emperor Constantine saw a cross of light in the sky. He thought it was a sign from Christ. He won the battle and believed that Christ had helped him.

SECRET WORSHIP

Despite the risks, groups of Christians would meet in secret in Rome. It was only in 312 CE that Emperor Constantine allowed Christians to worship openly.

Christianity began to gain in popularity, and eventually replaced the old gods and goddesses. Emperor Julian tried to bring back worshiping these gods and goddesses but was unsuccessful. Eventually, Christianity became the official religion of the Roman Empire.

MYTH LINKS

It is thought that many of the important dates in the Christian religion were set to overshadow festivals from the old beliefs. For example, the dates for Christmas and Easter competed with the festivals of the Sun god and the spring festivals.

Influence

Myths and legends offered the ancient Romans hope and reassurance that there were greater beings that could influence their lives. By worshiping these gods and goddesses, the Romans thought they could ensure a better harvest or victory in battle.

ROMAN LEGACY

When they conquered new territories, the Romans not only found new gods to worship, but also spread their own beliefs. The names of Roman gods and goddesses appear in places you might not think of.

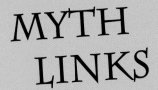

MYTH LINKS

Today, many people use Roman gods or goddesses in the names of their businesses or products:

- The Hercules transport plane is used to carry large or heavy cargo.
- Venus is used in the name of many beauty products.

Can you think of any more examples?

MYTH LINKS

The Romans named the fifth day of the week after Jupiter. When the Anglo-Saxons began to use the Roman calendar, they called this day *Thunres-daeg*, which stands for "Thor's day." Thor was their thunder god, so he was the equivalent to the Romans' Jupiter.

We still use the Roman calendar today. According to Roman legend, this was set by Romulus, the founder of Rome. He divided the year into 10 months and gave some of them names in honor of the gods. March was called *Martius*, meaning "month of Mars," and June was named for the goddess Juno. A later emperor added two more months, one of which was January, named after the god Janus.

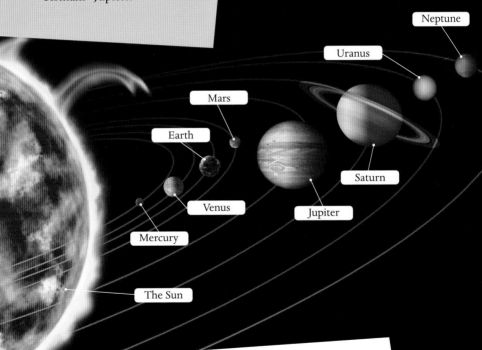

Neptune

Uranus

Mars

Earth

Saturn

Venus

Jupiter

Mercury

The Sun

Did you know?

You can see the influence of Roman myths in the sky. Planets such as Venus, Mars, Mercury, and Jupiter are named after Roman gods.

Characters, Creatures, and Places

Look at the words in brackets to find out how to say these Roman names.

GODS AND GODDESSES

Apollo god of the Sun, medicine, music, poetry, and philosophy, son of Jupiter

Bacchus (Back-us) god of wine

Ceres goddess of crops and harvests

Cupid god of love

Diana goddess of hunting

Isis (I-sis) goddess from Egypt, popular throughout the Roman Empire

Janus god of doorways and new beginnings

Juno goddess of marriage and childbirth, wife and sister of Jupiter

Jupiter supreme ruler of the gods

Lares (lair-riz) household protector gods

Maia goddess of fertility and spring

Mars god of war, son of the goddess Juno, father of Romulus and Remus

Mercury god of thieves and trade, son of Jupiter

Minerva goddess of wisdom, daughter of Jupiter

Mithras (Me-thras) god of light from Iran, popular with the Roman army

Neptune god of the sea

Olympians name given to the group of gods and goddesses living on Mount Olympus

Penates gods of the larder

Pluto god of the underworld

Prometheus (Pro-mee-thee-us) trickster, son of Lapetos

Tinia Etruscan god of thunder

Venus goddess of love, mother of Cupid and Aeneas

Vesta goddess of the fire in the hearth; also goddess of home and family

Vulcan god of fire, husband to Venus

HEROES, MORTALS, AND OTHERS

Aeneas (Ay-nay-uhs) Trojan hero, ancestor of the founders of Rome, son of Venus

Anchises (An-ky-seez) mortal father of Aeneas

Argonauts crew of Jason's boat, the *Argo*

Castor and Pollux twin sons of Jupiter, accompanied Jason on the *Argo*

Dido queen of Carthage

Gaius Mucius Scaevola (Guy-us Mu-kee-us Sky-vo-la) a Roman youth, famous for his bravery

Hercules son of Jupiter and human mother Alcmena; a heroic mortal who was made a god after his death

Idas and Lynceus (I-das) (Lie-n-see-us) twin brothers who fought against Castor and Pollux

Jason legendary Greek hero and leader of the Argonauts

Rhea Silvia priestess, mother of Romulus and Remus

Romulus and Remus founders of Rome, twin sons of Mars and Rhea Silvia

Sibyl of Cumae priestess who could predict the future

AUTHORS

Apollonius of Rhodes poet who wrote of the mythological story of Jason and the Argonauts

Gaius Valerius Flaccus (Guy-us Val-er-ee-us Flack-us) Roman poet who wrote an epic poem based on Apollonius's *Argonautica*

Livy Roman historian, born Titus Livius in about 59 BCE

Ovid Roman poet, born Publius Ovidius Naso in 43 BCE

Virgil Roman poet who wrote *The Aeneid*, which tells the story of Aeneas and the founding of Rome

CREATURES

Cerberus the three-headed dog that guards the underworld

Cyclops one-eyed giant from Sicily

PLACES

Capitoline Hill place in Rome where the Capitoline Temple buildings are and where the Roman government is based

Carthage city in North Africa

Cumae (Coo-mee) Greek colony

Elysian Fields (El-ee-see-an) place in the underworld for the souls of the good

Mount Etna volcano in Sicily, Italy, said to be where Vulcan made his forge

Mount Olympus mountain in Greece believed to be the home of the gods

Pantheon temple in Rome built to worship all gods

Rome capital city of Italy

Sicily island off the coast of Italy

Tiber River river in Italy upon which Rome stands

Troy legendary city, thought to be on the Turkish coast

Glossary

altar table or flat block used as a place to make offerings or sacrifices to the gods

Anglo-Saxons people who lived in England until the Norman Conquest in 1066

attribute quality or characteristic associated with a person or god

blacksmith person who makes things out of iron

Celtic relating to the Celts, who were a tribe of people including the Irish, Scottish, and Welsh

commerce act of buying and selling

conquer take control of a place or people by force

constellation group of stars in the sky that form a pattern or picture

cosmic relating to the universe or cosmos, rather than Earth

cult religious devotion to a particular person or object

descendant someone who is related to a particular person who lived in the past

emperor ruler of an empire

epic long poem telling of the adventures of heroic figures

Etruscans people who controlled an area of Italy, north of the Tiber River

famine long period of time with little or no food. People often die from lack of food during a famine.

folktale traditional story told by a people

forge blacksmith's workshop

hearth floor of a fireplace

immortal living forever; describes a being who cannot be killed

lyre stringed musical instrument

mortal human being that will not live forever

persecute treat someone badly, often because of their race or religion

philosophy study of the nature of knowledge and being

prophecy prediction of what will happen in the future

pyre fire for burning dead bodies as part of a funeral service

quest long, difficult search for something

Roman Empire empire that succeeded the Roman Republic. It was established in about 27 BCE.

sacred connected with a god or other divine power

sacrifice act of killing an animal or person as an offering to a god or goddess

slave person who is owned by another and is not free to do as they choose

superstitious believing in magic and luck

temple place of worship or home for a god or goddess

trickster character in myths who plays tricks and makes mischief

underworld place where the souls of the dead were believed to go

Find Out More

BOOKS

Daning, Tom. *Roman Mythology: Romulus and Remus* (Jr. Graphic Mythologies). New York: Rosen Classroom, 2006.

Innes, Brian. *Ancient Roman Myths* (Myths from Around the World). New York: Gareth Stevens, 2010.

Lunge-Larsen, Lise. *Gifts from the Gods: Ancient Words and Wisdom from Greek and Roman Mythology.* Boston: Houghton Mifflin, 2011.

Orr, Tamra. *The Monsters of Hercules* (Monsters in Myth). Hockessin, Del.: Mitchell Lane Publishers, 2010.

Spires, Elizabeth. *I Am Arachne: Fifteen Greek and Roman Myths.* New York: Square Fish, 2009.

WEB SITES

www.metmuseum.org/toah/hd/roem/hd_roem.htm
Learn more about the Roman Empire and see some artifacts at this Metropolitan Museum of Art web site.

www.museumnetworkuk.org/myths
Explore more about Greek and Roman myths.

www.pantheon.org
Encyclopedia Mythica is an encyclopedia of mythology, folklore, and religion.

www.pbs.org/empires/romans/empire/index.html
This PBS web site discusses the Roman Empire in the first century CE and accompanies a TV series on the topic.

www.rome.mrdonn.org
This web site has many links to information about ancient Rome.

DVDS

Hercules (Disney, 1997).

   This film tells the tale of the Roman hero Hercules.

History Classics: Ancient Rome (A&E Home Video, 2010).

When Rome Ruled (National Geographic Video, 2011).

PLACES TO VISIT

Use the Internet to find places to visit where you can learn more about Roman myths and Roman life. Perhaps your local museum has a collection of Roman artifacts that you could investigate?

The Metropolitan Museum of Art
1000 Fifth Avenue
New York, NY 10028-0198
www.metmuseum.org
Explore the Greek and Roman galleries to see some of the 17,000 works in the Met's collection from those ancient cultures.

Museum of Fine Arts Boston
Avenue of the Arts
465 Huntington Avenue
Boston, MA 02115
www.mfa.org
Sample this museum's impressive collection of artifacts from the ancient world.

FURTHER RESEARCH

Are you interested in how the Roman Empire was founded and how it conquered more land? You could use your local library and the Internet to find out more. The Romans adopted many myths from the Greeks, so you could research some more of these Greek myths. Perhaps you are interested in quests and adventures? You could research the 12 labors of Hercules and discover what challenges he was given. Or you could explore the fascinating monsters that the Greeks believed in.

Index